**SUPERGRASS**
*LIFE ON OTHER PLANETS*
GUITAR TABLATURE VOCAL

PUBLISHED 2002
© INTERNATIONAL MUSIC PUBLICATIONS LIMITED
GRIFFIN HOUSE, 161 HAMMERSMITH ROAD, LONDON, W6 8BS, ENGLAND.

EDITED BY CHRIS HARVEY.
MUSIC ARRANGED BY ARTEMIS MUSIC LTD.
ALL ART MADE IN THE DESIGNERS REPUBLIC.

# ZA

WORDS AND MUSIC BY GARETH COOMBES, MICHAEL QUINN, DANIEL GOFFEY AND ROBERT COOMBES

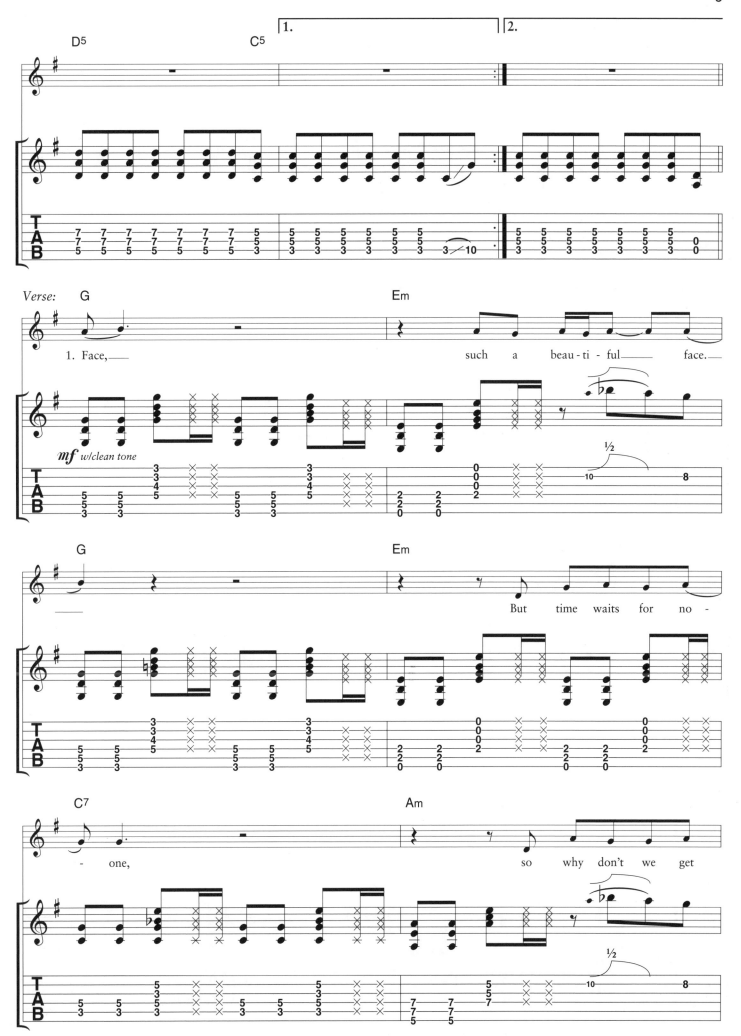

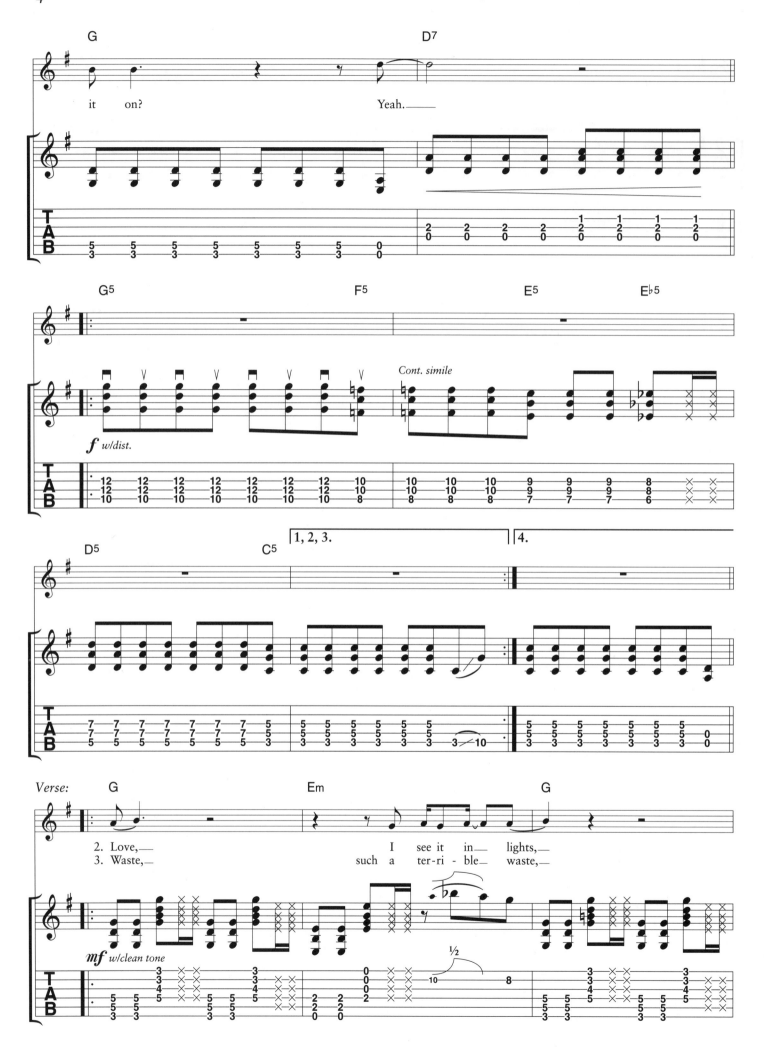

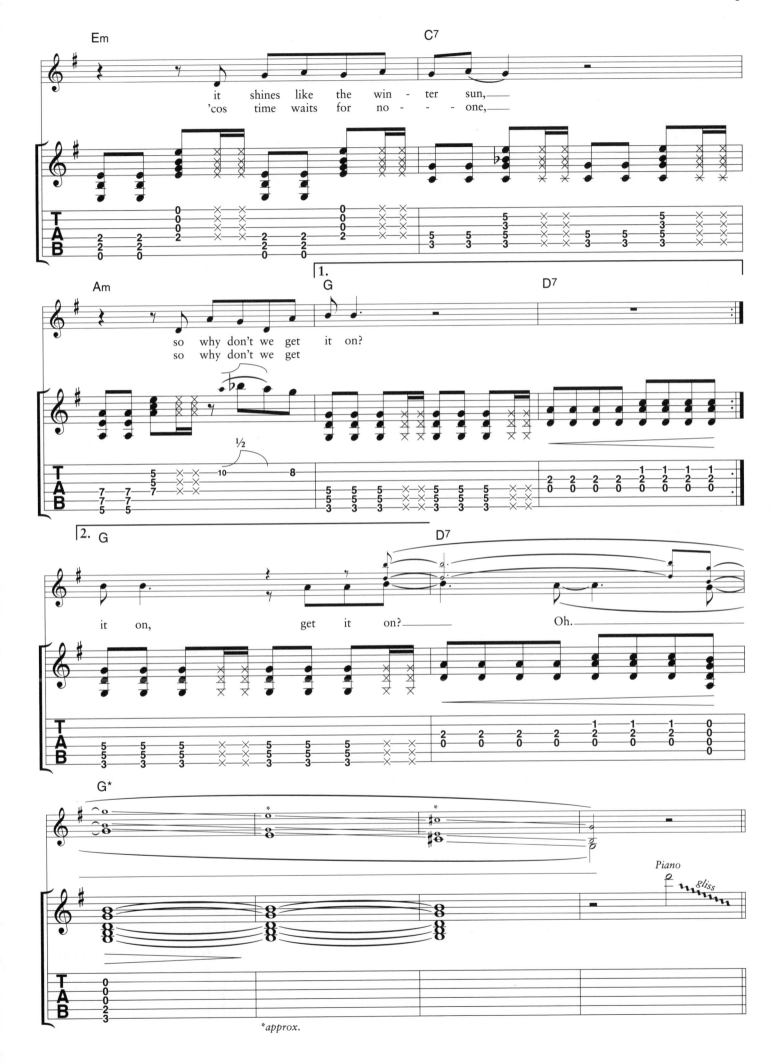

it shines like the win- ter sun,
'cos time waits for no- - one,

so why don't we get it on?
so why don't we get

it on, get it on? Oh.

*approx.

Fig. 2

# RUSH HOUR SOUL

### WORDS AND MUSIC BY GARETH COOMBES, MICHAEL QUINN, DANIEL GOFFEY AND ROBERT COOMBES

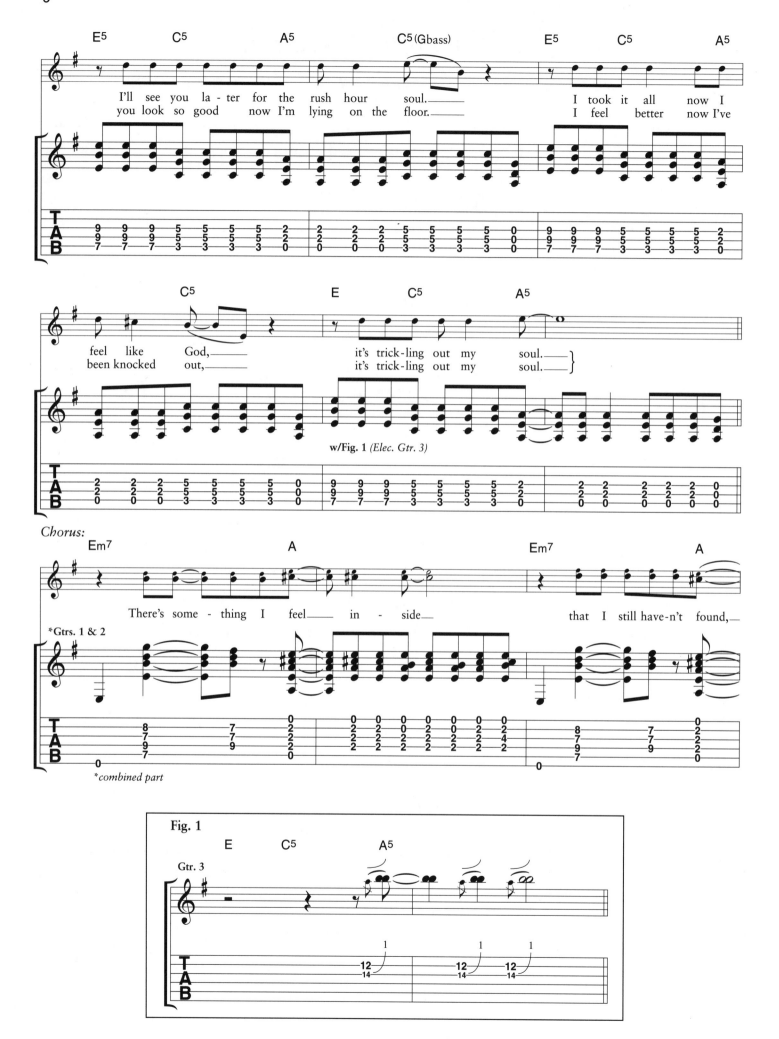

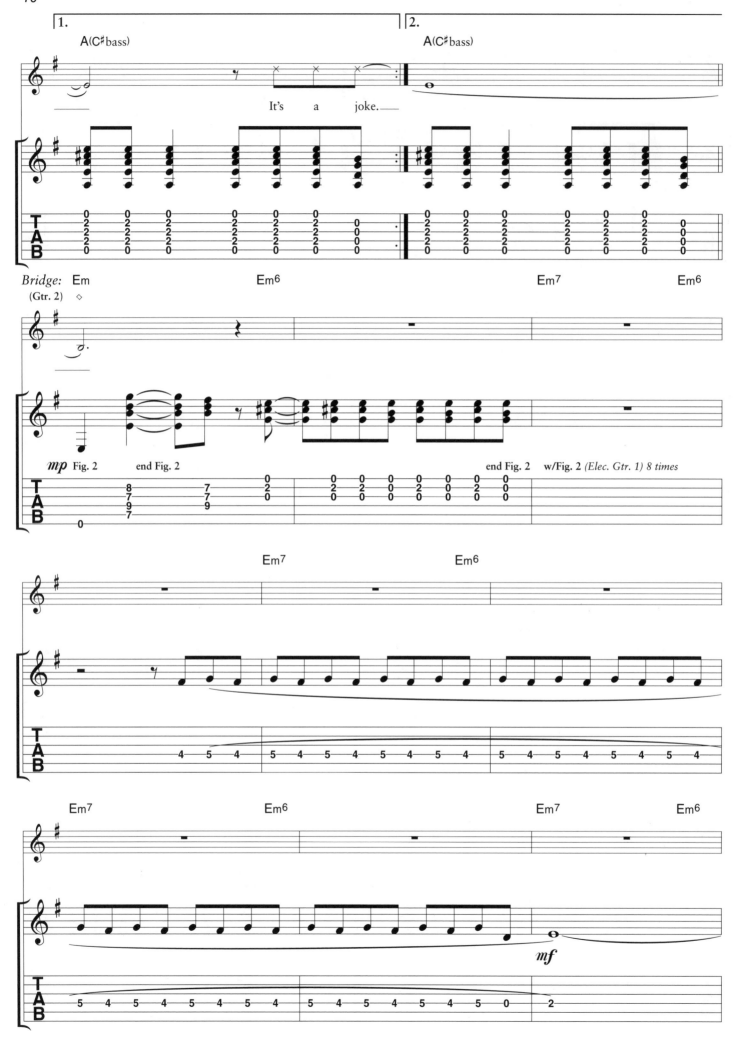

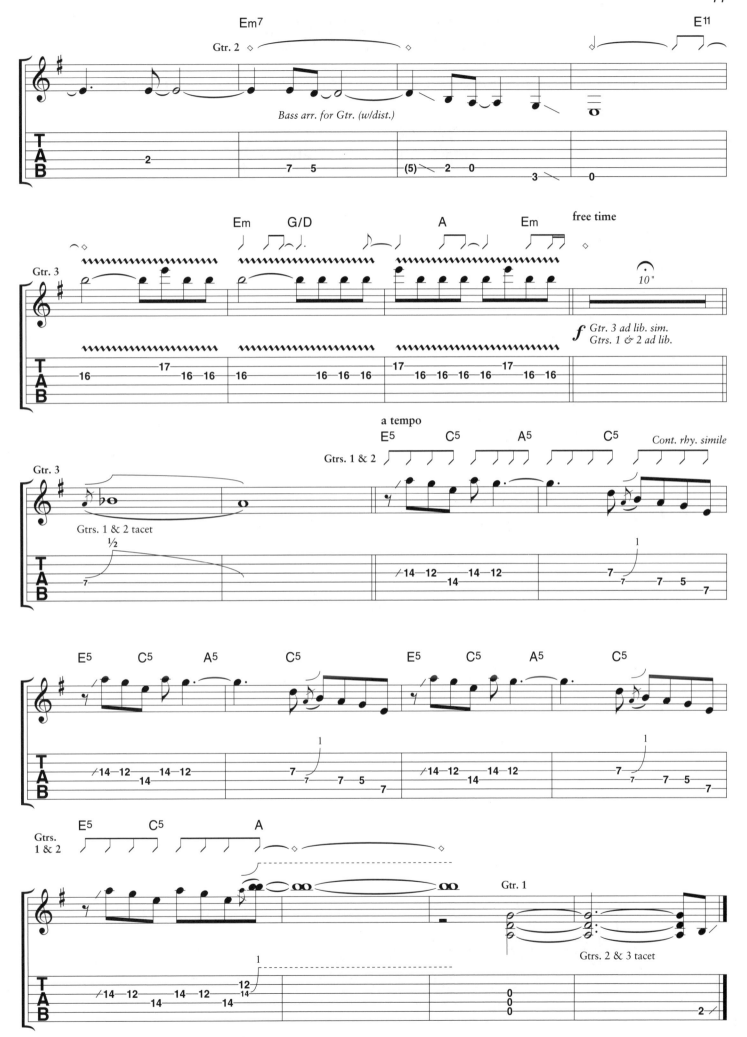

# SEEN THE LIGHT

*WORDS AND MUSIC BY GARETH COOMBES, MICHAEL QUINN, DANIEL GOFFEY AND ROBERT COOMBES*

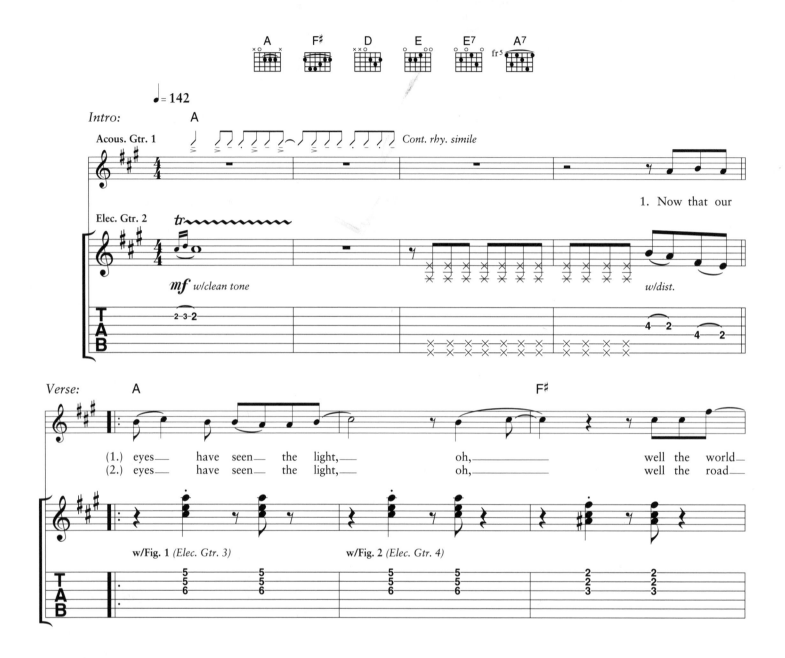

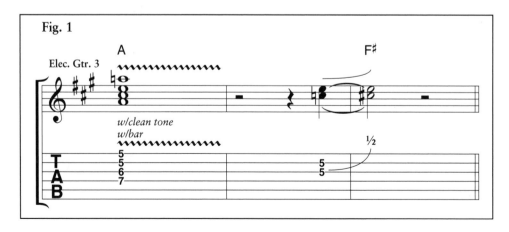

Fig. 2

# BRECON BEACONS

*WORDS AND MUSIC BY GARETH COOMBES, MICHAEL QUINN, DANIEL GOFFEY AND ROBERT COOMBES*

Fig. 1

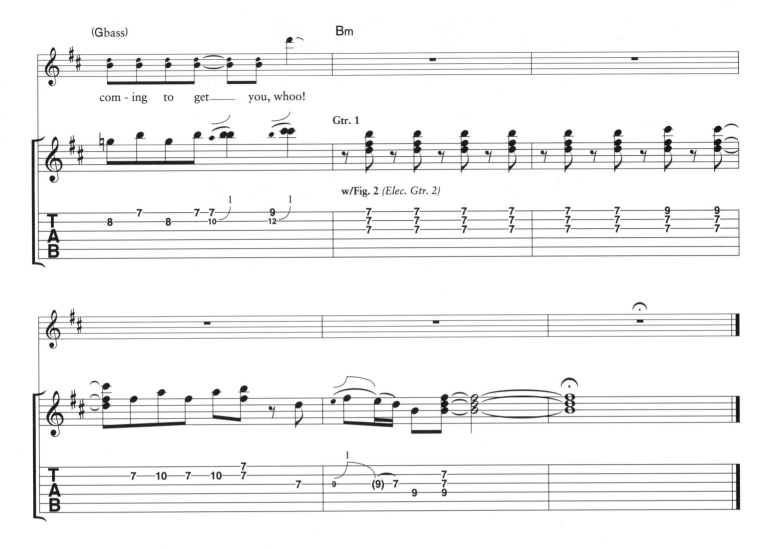

(Gbass)     Bm

com - ing   to   get____   you, whoo!

Gtr. 1

w/Fig. 2 *(Elec. Gtr. 2)*

**Fig. 2**

Gtr. 2     Bm

*Verse 3:*
Well she took her last gasp
As the town was sleeping
While the finger pointed to a local policeman.

Well the juries are still out *etc.*

# CAN'T GET UP

WORDS AND MUSIC BY GARETH COOMBES, MICHAEL QUINN, DANIEL GOFFEY AND ROBERT COOMBES

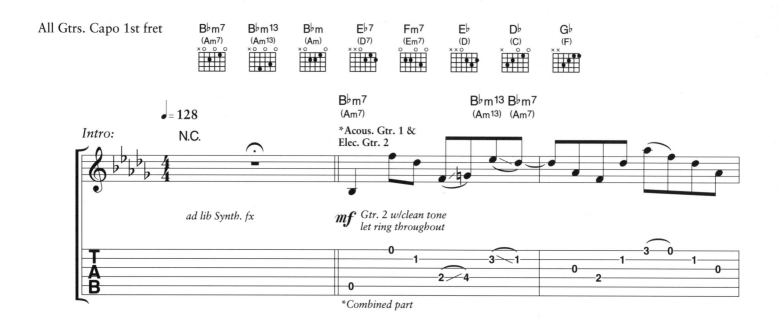

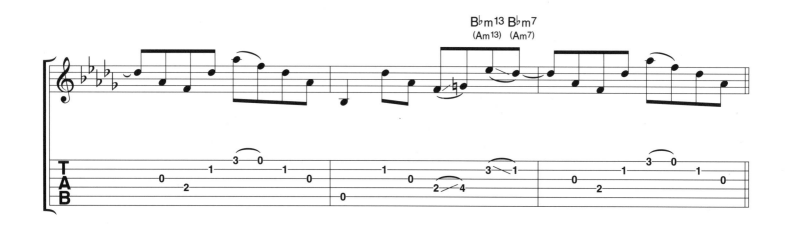

23

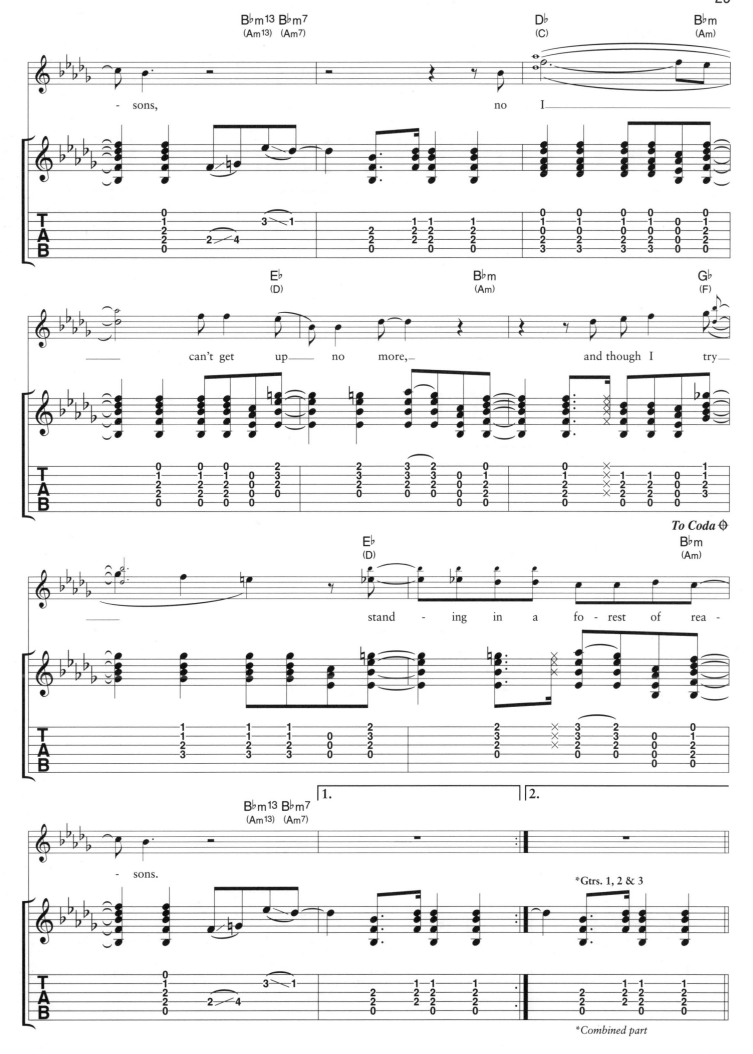

# EVENING OF THE DAY

### WORDS AND MUSIC BY GARETH COOMBES, MICHAEL QUINN, DANIEL GOFFEY AND ROBERT COOMBES

1. 'Tis the eve - ning of the day,
3. Is this a part - ing of the ways,

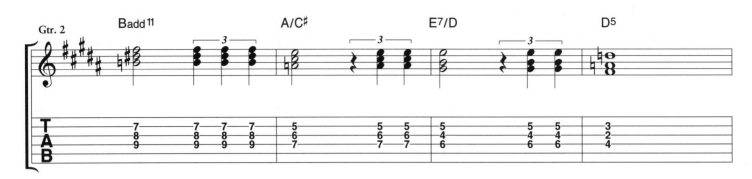

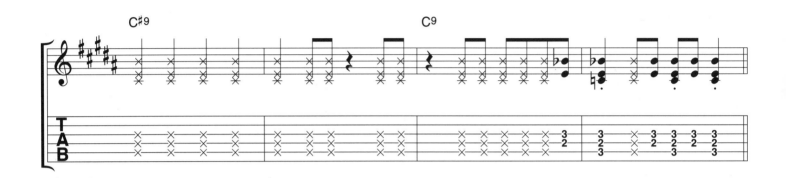

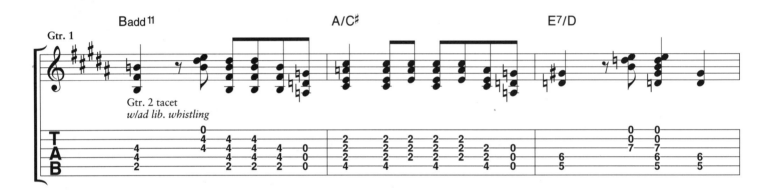

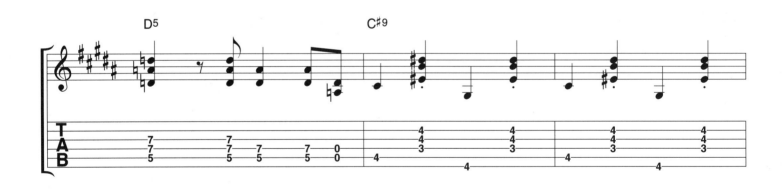

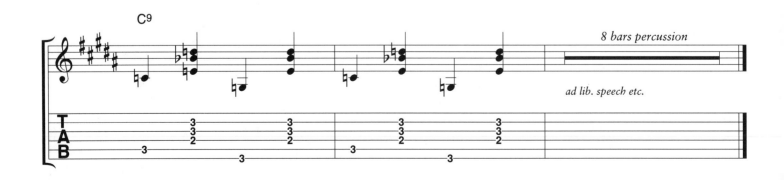

# NEVER DONE NOTHING LIKE THAT BEFORE

WORDS AND MUSIC BY GARETH COOMBES, MICHAEL QUINN, DANIEL GOFFEY AND ROBERT COOMBES

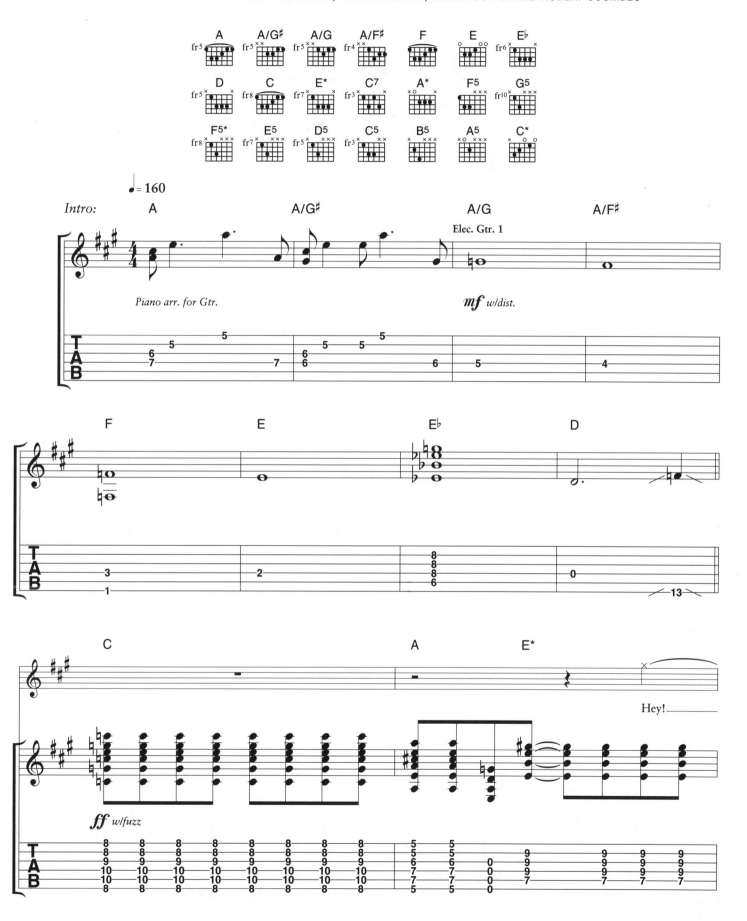

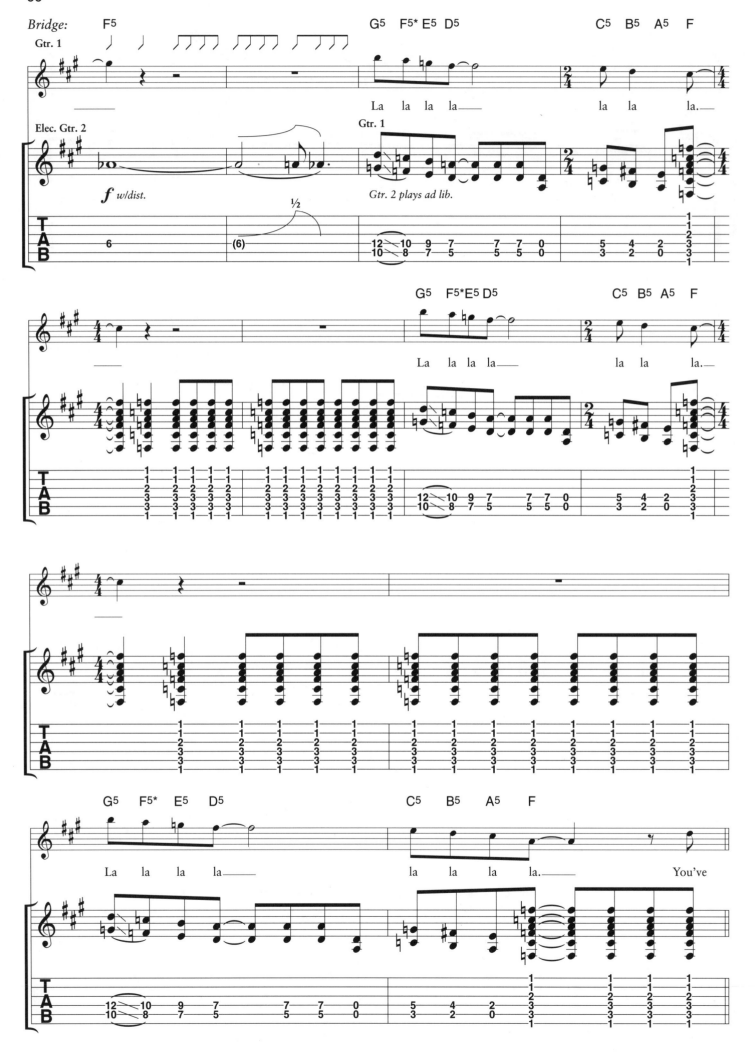

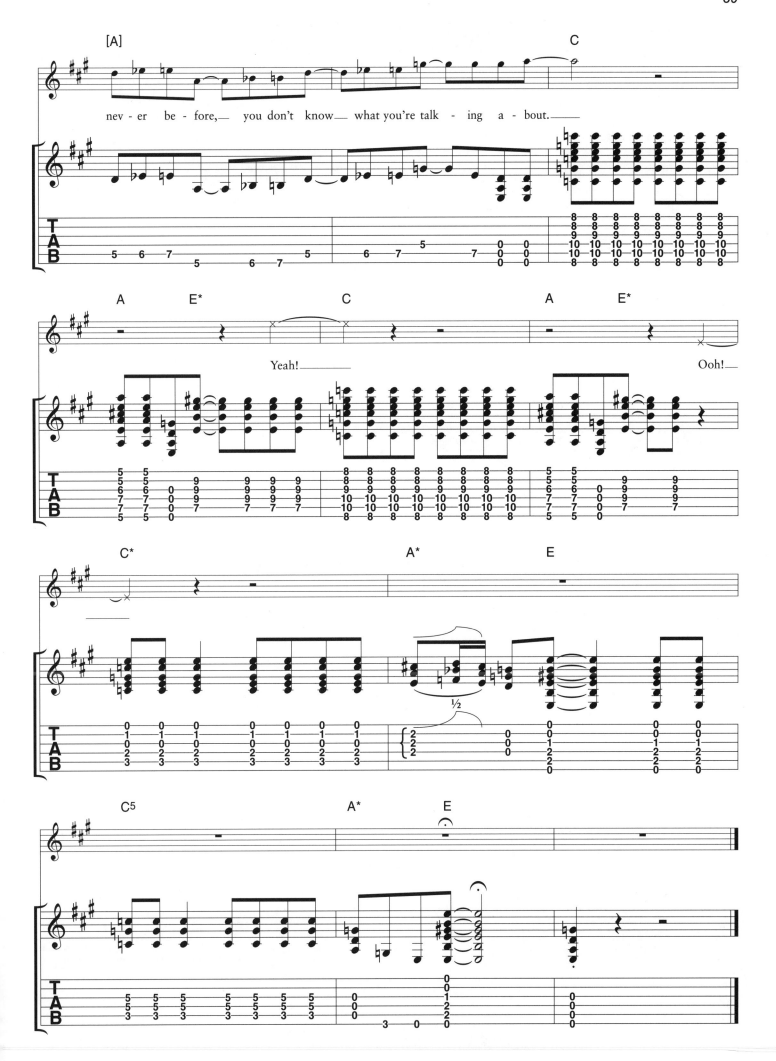

# FUNNIEST THING

### WORDS AND MUSIC BY GARETH COOMBES, MICHAEL QUINN, DANIEL GOFFEY AND ROBERT COOMBES

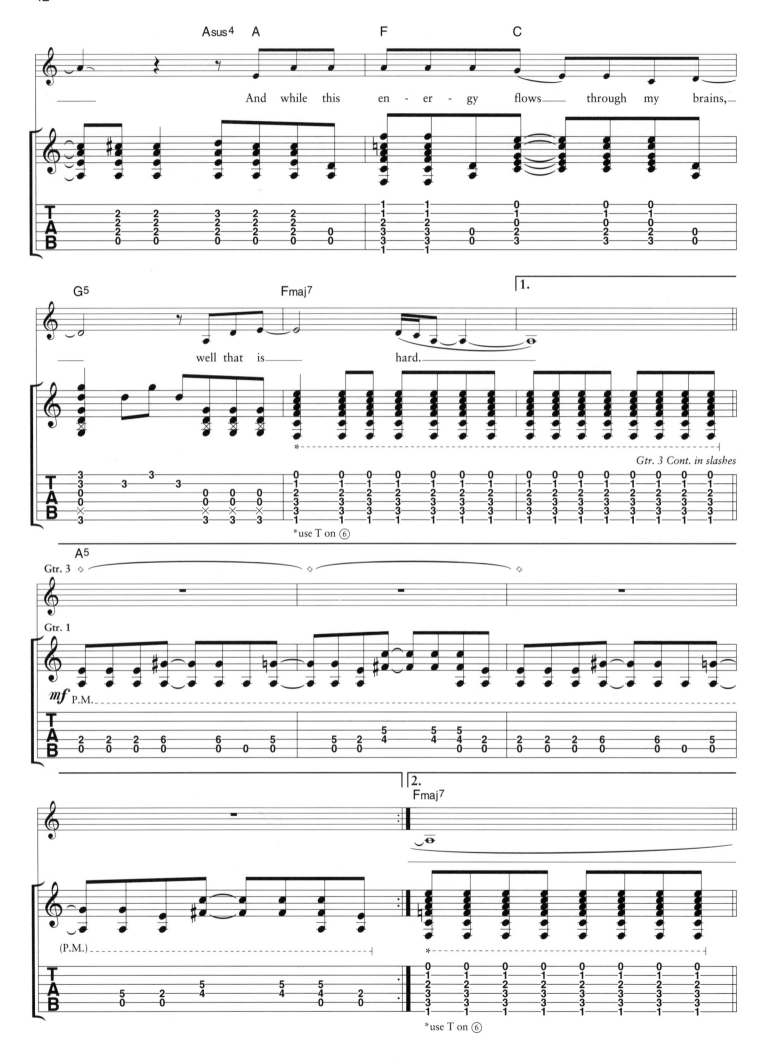

And while this en-er-gy flows through my brains,

well that is hard.

*use T on ⑥

Gtr. 3 Cont. in slashes

Gtr. 3

Gtr. 1

*use T on ⑥

And— it was the

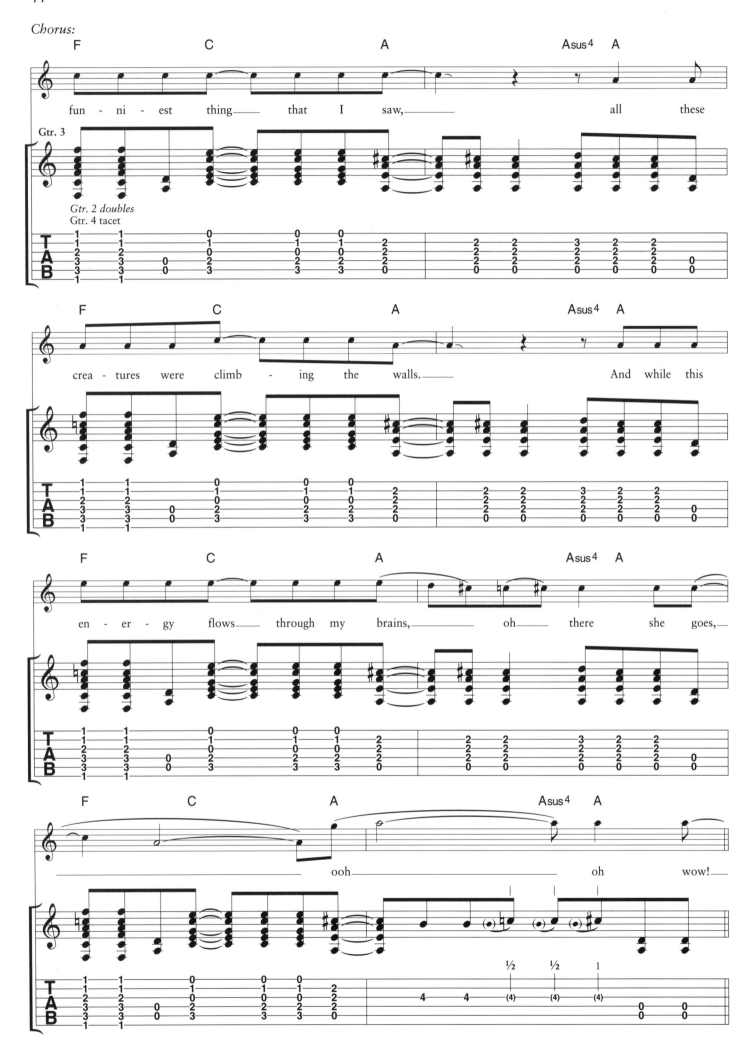

# GRACE

WORDS AND MUSIC BY GARETH COOMBES, MICHAEL QUINN, DANIEL GOFFEY AND ROBERT COOMBES

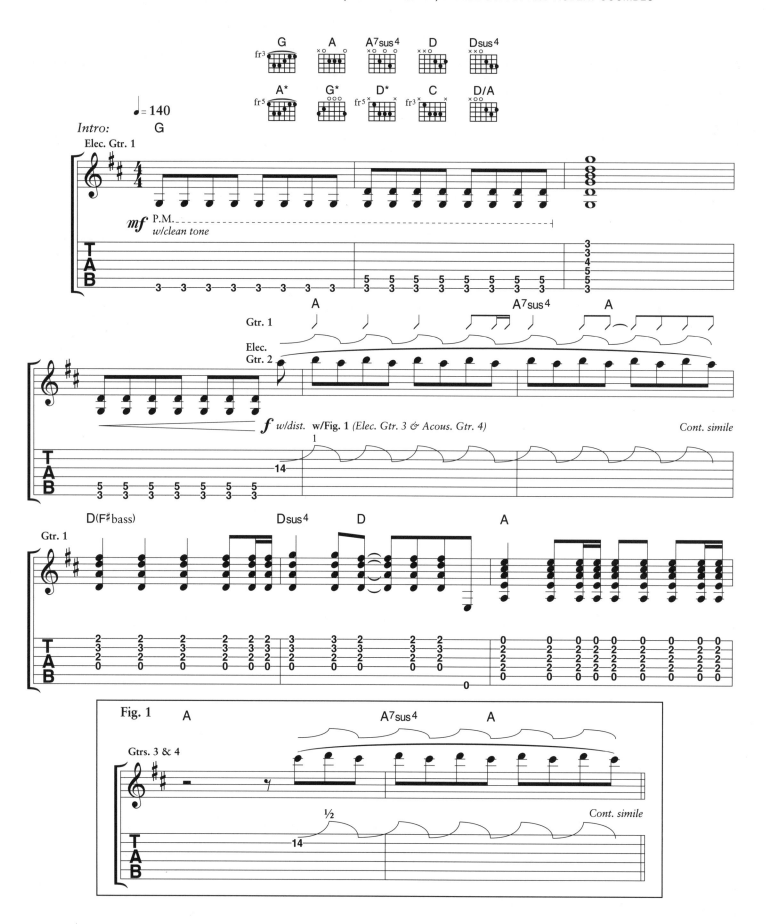

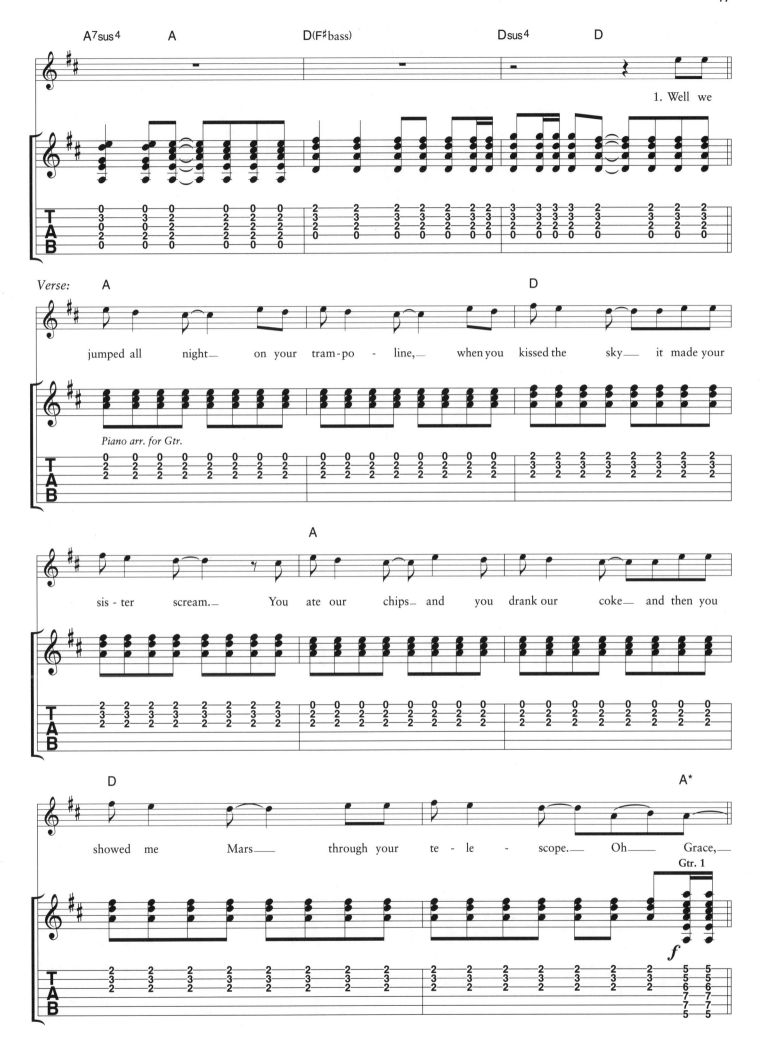

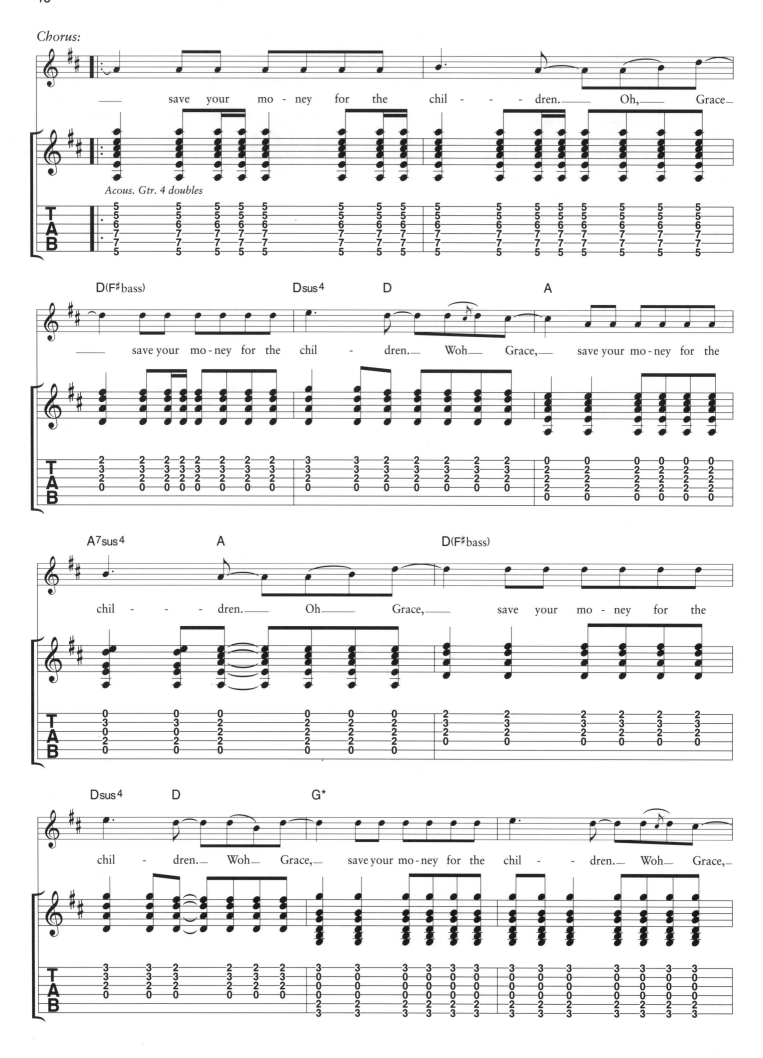

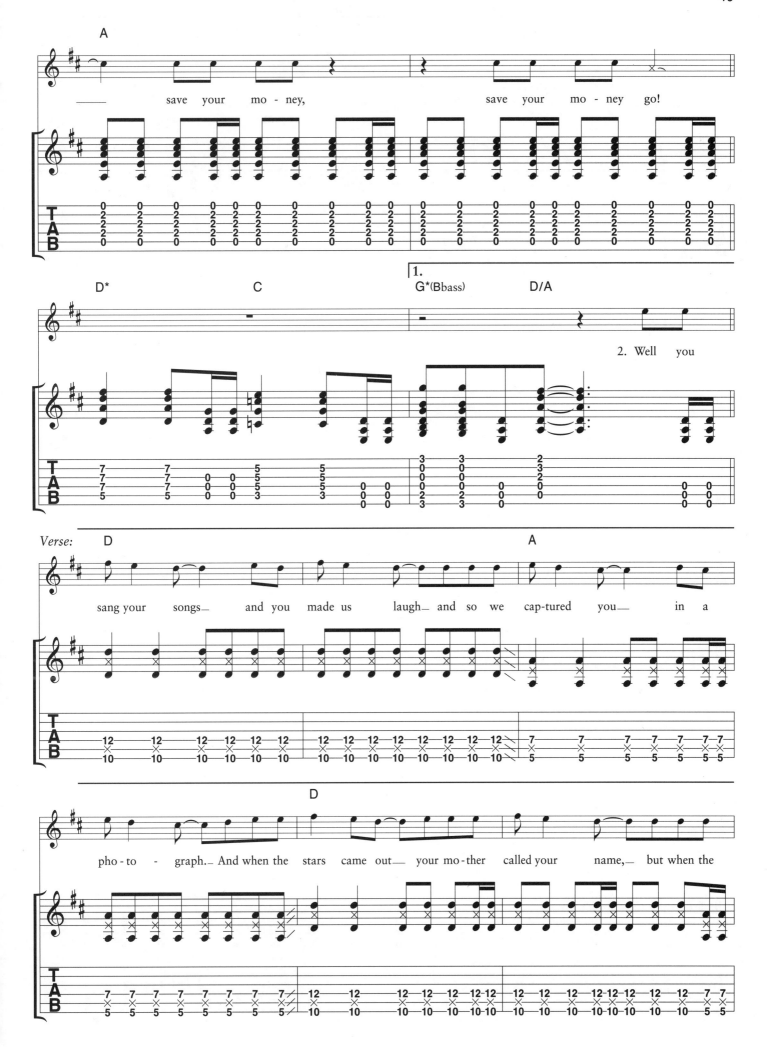

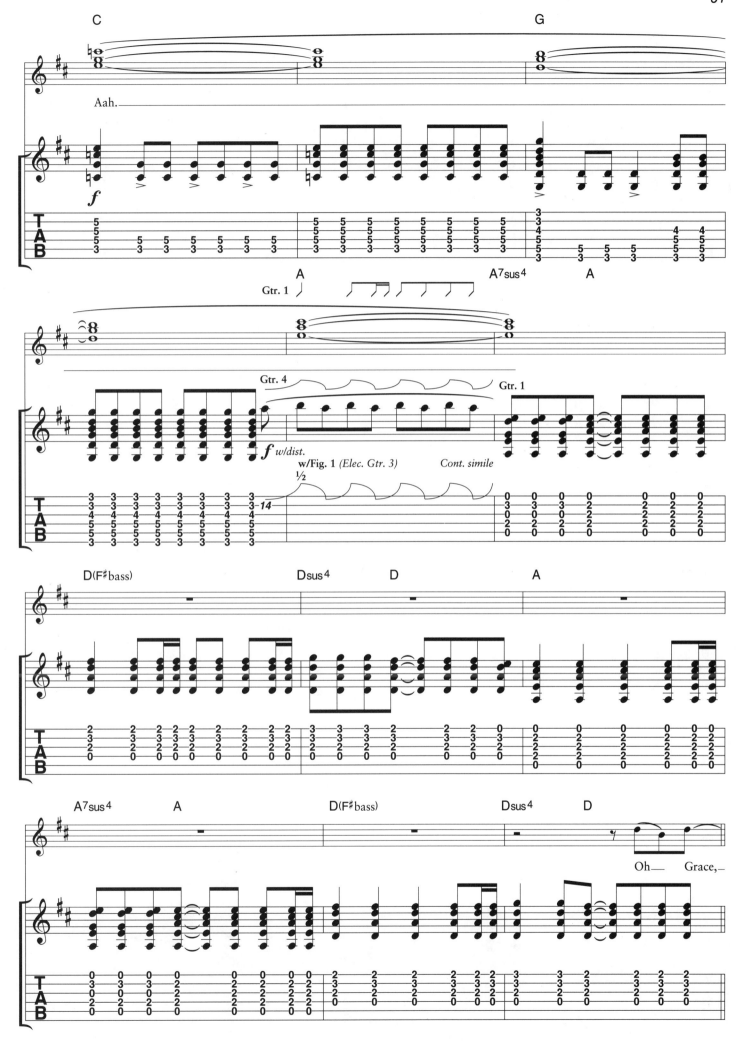

# PROPHET 15

### WORDS AND MUSIC BY GARETH COOMBES, MICHAEL QUINN, DANIEL GOFFEY AND ROBERT COOMBES

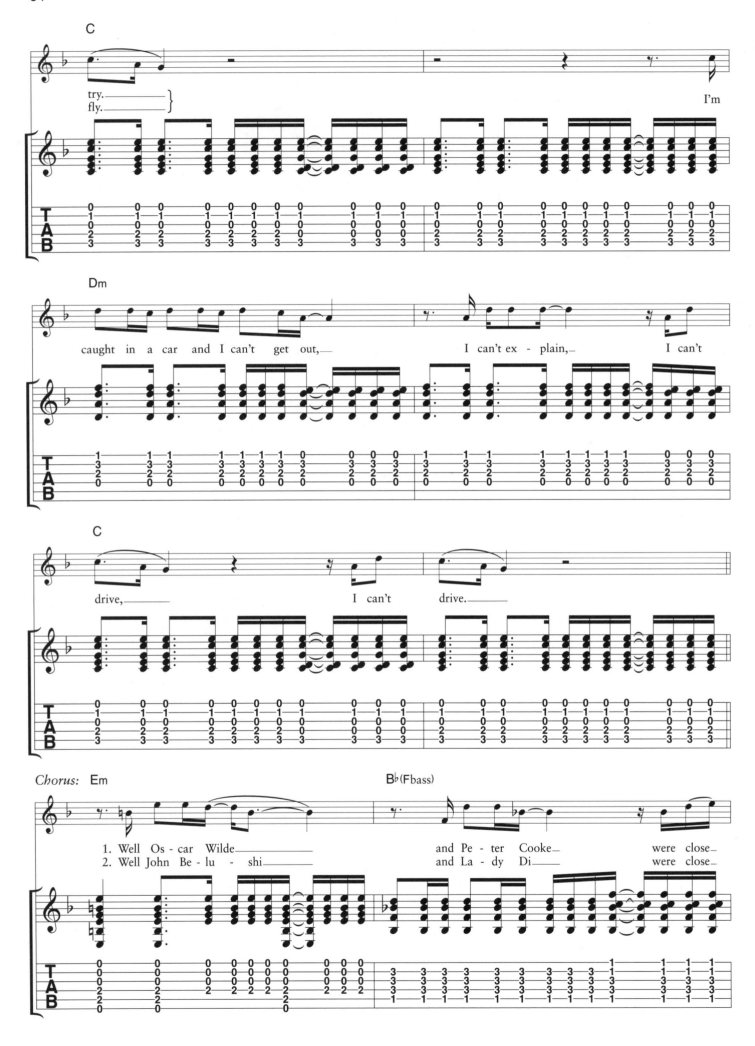

C

try.
fly.

I'm

Dm

caught in a car and I can't get out,——— I can't ex - plain,—— I can't

C

drive,——— I can't drive.———

*Chorus:* Em                                                    B♭(Fbass)

1. Well Os - car Wilde——— and Pe - ter Cooke—— were close——
2. Well John Be - lu - shi——— and La - dy Di—— were close——

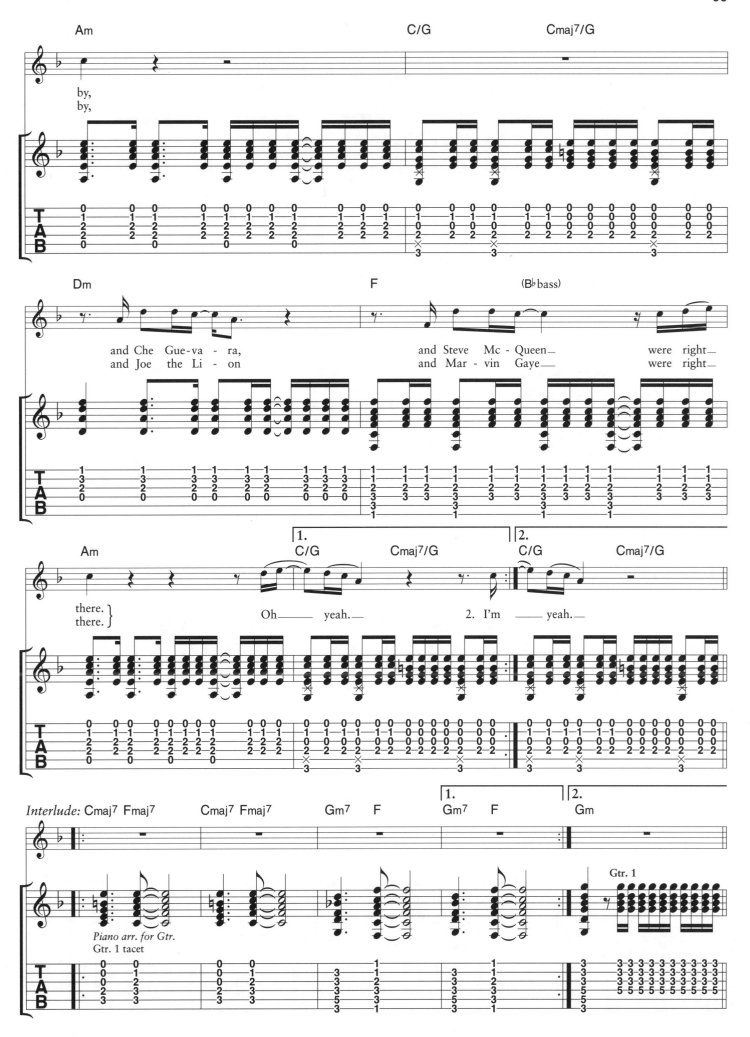

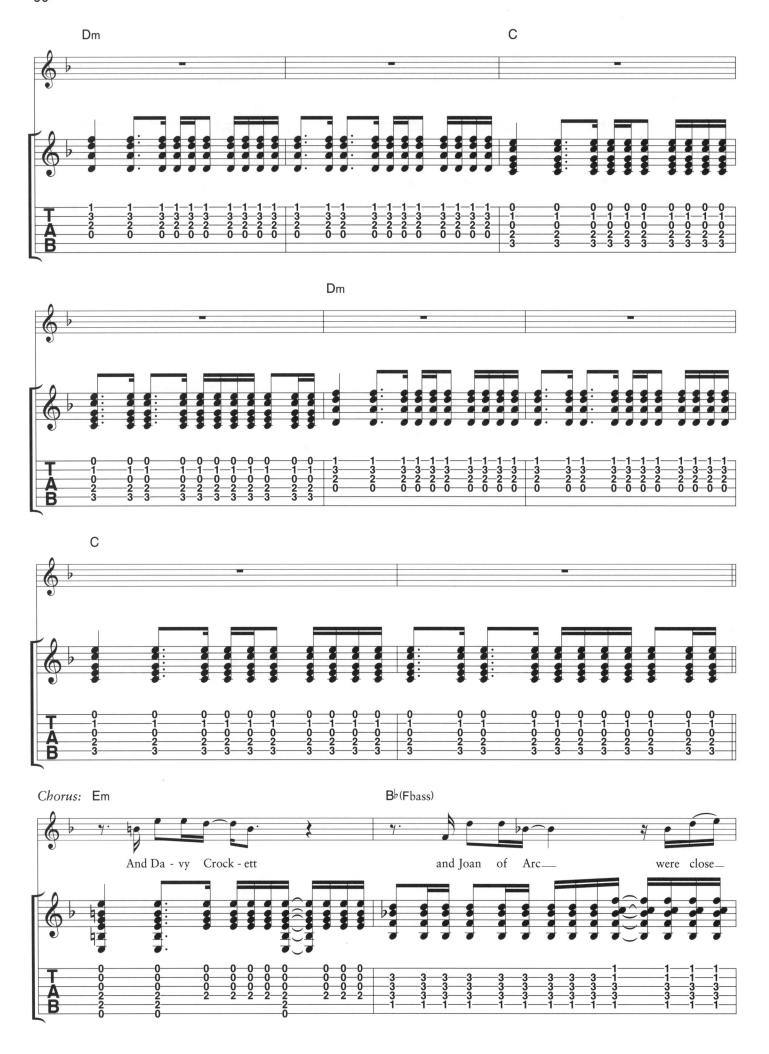

# LA SONG

### WORDS AND MUSIC BY GARETH COOMBES, MICHAEL QUINN, DANIEL GOFFEY AND ROBERT COOMBES

1. Well they

-bel, we'll do the dance of the mashed po-ta-to. Well they

*Interlude:*

*Elec. Gtr. 3*

Harm.

*mf w/clean tone*

Harm. Harm.

*Gtr. 4 plays backwards ad lib.*

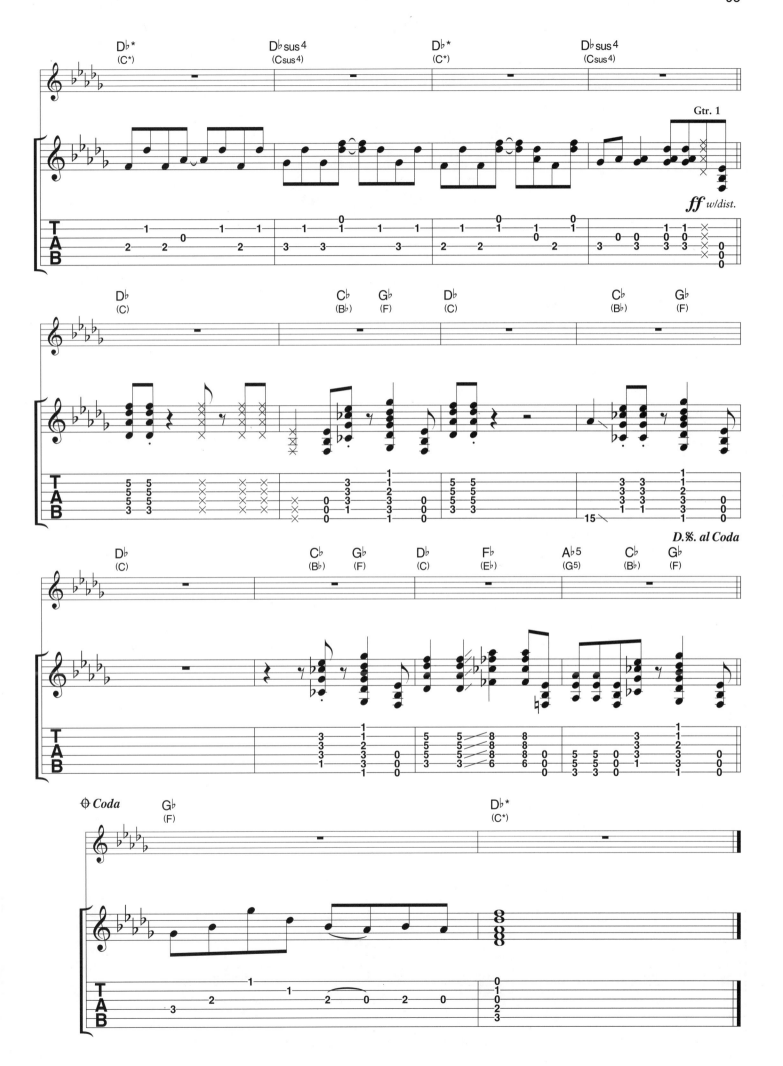

# RUN

WORDS AND MUSIC BY GARETH COOMBES, MICHAEL QUINN, DANIEL GOFFEY AND ROBERT COOMBES

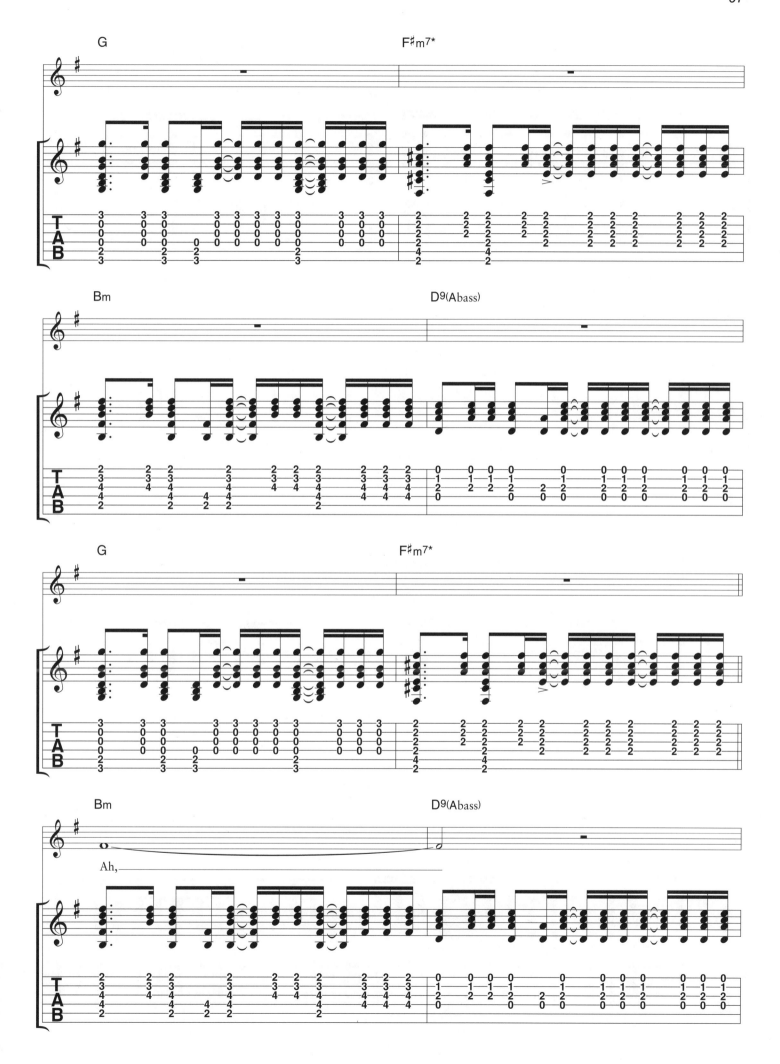

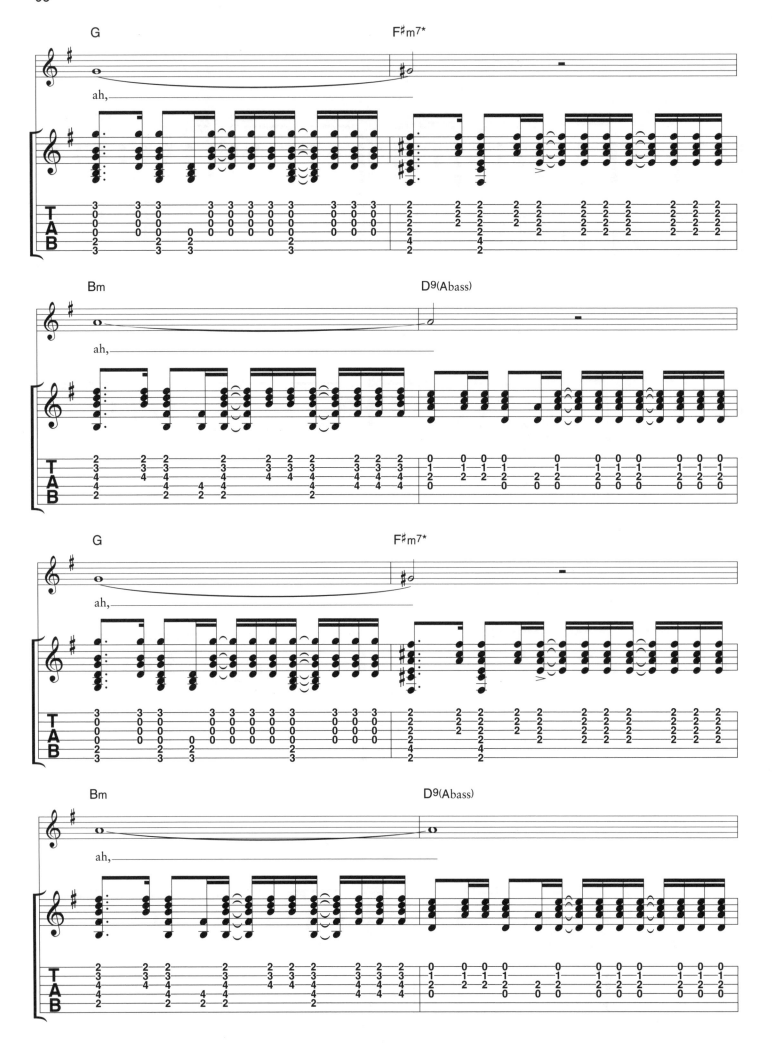

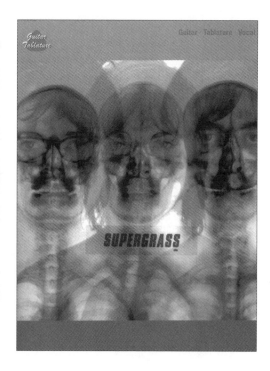